How to Be a SwagMaster

T. Cathers-Mitchell

How to Be a SwagMaster

Copyright © 2019 by T. Cathers-Mitchell

All rights reserved. No part of this publication may be reproduced, distributed, or transmitted in any form or by any means, including photocopying, recording, or other electronic or mechanical methods, without the prior written permission of the publisher, except in the case of brief quotations embodied in critical reviews and certain other noncommercial uses permitted by copyright law.

Table of Contents

Introduction	**4**
What is Swagbucks?	**5**
How to Get Started	**7**
Ways to Earn SBs	**9**
Apps and Games	**15**
Tips and Tricks	**20**
Conclusion	**28**
References	**29**

Introduction

What is a SwagMaster? A SwagMaster is a person who has mastered the art of earning cash and gift cards online via Swagbucks.com. I have been on Swagbucks for just over one year now and have already earned over $500 in gift cards and cash payments via PayPal.

I wrote this book to show you how you can become a SwagMaster too. I must, however, begin with this disclaimer:

Swagbucks is not a get rich quick scheme. On a good day I will earn $3 to $5. However, those few extra dollars per day do add up quickly.

This last winter over a six-week period, I was able to earn over $200 toward Christmas, which was a big help! I know that doesn't seem like much but earning just one dollar per day adds up to $30 per month that you didn't have before.

This book is packed with all the information you need to learn how to use Swagbucks like a pro. I have included several tips and tricks and all my insider knowledge on how to earn cash and gift cards quickly and easily.

Anyway, I'm a fan of keeping things short and sweet. I hope that you find this book informative and interesting and I'm looking forward to turning you all into SwagMasters like me!

What is Swagbucks?

Swagbucks.com is one of the web's most popular rewards programs. It is a website and search engine where you can earn points called Swagbucks (SB) for things that you already do online. Swagbucks is owned and operated by Prodege LLC, and based in El Segundo, California.

Swagbucks was founded in 2005 and has over 60 million registered members, and over 2.4 million Facebook fans. They have awarded over 500 million dollars in rewards to their members.

On Swagbucks.com you can earn points for simply searching the web, shopping, completing offers, watching videos and filling out surveys.

Each point that you earn on Swagbucks.com is called a Swagbuck (SB) and is worth about one cent. Swagbucks can be redeemed for gift cards or cash or can be used to enter sweepstakes or even be donated to charity.

Swagbucks can be redeemed in increments of as low as $3.00 (300 SBs) for an Amazon gift card or even for cash via PayPal in increments as low as $25.00 (2500 SBs).

I should also note that Swagbucks is not a get rich quick scheme. While you can earn money and gift cards on Swagbucks, please don't quit your day jobs! Swagbucks will not bring in enough money to sustain you, but it is a fun way to earn a few extra bucks!

How to Get Started

Now that you know a little bit about Swagbucks, here's how to get started. First you need to go to Swagbucks.com and create an account. You can either enter all your info into the form to click sign up with Facebook, which makes the process a little easier.

Once you have signed up, you may have to verify your email address by clicking a link in your welcome email. After you confirm your email address, you are all set, and you can begin earning SB like a pro!

You may want to take a few moments just exploring Swagbucks.com and seeing just how many ways you can earn SBs.

You can begin earning SBs in many ways. I suggest trying a survey or watching your first set of videos, but you can also check out the special offers, do a little shopping, etc. If you get lost, you can always click on the "How It Works under Quick Links toward the bottom of the page on the left. The next chapter will tell you all about how to earn your first SB. Happy Swagging!

Ways to Earn SBs

Swagbucks.com offers many ways to earn Swagbucks (SB).

- Searching the web - Swagbucks has its own search engine and will award bonus SB by giving you a code to enter after several searches. Your SBs are awarded when you enter the code, and you can continue searching the web without further interruptions. You can earn even more SB from searching the web when you make Swagbucks your default web browser.
- Shopping - Swagbucks offers cash back in the form of SB from thousands of stores online like Amazon, Target and Wal-Mart.

- SB from shopping are usually shown as pending for 30 days.
- Completing offers - You can earn SB for completing offers like signing up for Hulu, printing coupons and downloading and installing games on your mobile devices.
- Playing games - Swagbucks has fun games, like Swago (which is their version of Bingo), Swag IQ (a live online trivia game) or SB Bowling.
- Watching videos - You can earn SB (up to 500 SB daily) by simply watching videos either on their website or on their many video apps for both iPhone and Android.
- Doing surveys – One of the most fun (and most profitable) ways to earn SB is by completing surveys either online or on their Answer app.

- Swagstakes – SB can be used to enter sweepstakes to win a wide variety of prizes from more SB to game systems, tablets and more.
- Referrals - You can earn 300 SBs for referring a friend to Swagbucks, as well as 10% of their earnings for the life of their account. You will also receive 100 SBs when someone that you referred adds Swagbutton to their computer.
- Swag Codes - Swagbucks will send you notifications telling you when there is a swag code available. When you see a notification for a swag code and you click on it you will be brought to a site with a swag code, which you can enter on Swagbucks.com, Swagbutton or SB Mobile for some bonus SB.

- Daily Goals and Monthly Bonuses - Your daily goal meter shows up at the top of your home page and when you hover your pointer over it, your daily goal will show as well as how many SBs you will earn if you meet that goal. Your daily goals come in two tiers. Once you meet your first goal, another will show up with a higher SB bonus for meeting it. Earnings from your daily goals make up your monthly bonus, which you can claim when it shows under your daily goal meter each month.
- To Do List - Your To Do List refreshes each day and can be found on your home page on Swagbucks.com. You get bonus SB every time you complete your To Do List. Tasks on your To Do List include" voting in the Daily Poll, clicking on Daily

- Search, viewing the Deal of the Day, completing an offer in Discover, and attempting and completing a survey.
- SwagUps - A SwagUp is a bonus or that Swagbucks applies to your account. The bonus that you receive from the SwagUp depends on the type that is applied to your account. There are two types of Swag Ups: a reward SwagUp and a rebate Swag Up. An award SwagUp adds SBs to your account when you complete the activities that unlock the award. A rebate SwagUp gives you an SB rebate when you redeem you SBs for a gift card.

Once you've earned enough SB, you can redeem them for gift cards or cash via PayPal. There are a lot of different gift cards to choose from. The most popular ones are the $5 Amazon gift card for 500 SBs or the $3 Amazon gift card for 300 SB, or PayPal cash deposits starting at $25 for 2500 SBs.

Apps and Games

Swagbucks has several different games and mobile apps with which you can earn SB:

- Swago - Swago is Swagbucks' own version of Bingo. You mark of your squares by completing the task inside that square. SB are awarded when you get a line, X, blackout, etc. The only catch is that you can only redeem your board for SB once per game, so it's best to wait until the end of the game period to redeem for your SB.
- Swag IQ – SwagIQ is Swagbucks' live trivia game. You can access the game via the SwagIQ app, available for both iPhone and Android. You can earn SB by answering questions right and split a grand prize if you get all the answers correct. You can

earn SB for correct answers, even if you get eliminated when you stay on until the end of the game to claim your SB.

- SB Bowling - SB Bowling is a simple little bowling game mobile app, available for both iPhone and Android. You roll the ball and knock down pins, just like a normal bowling game and earn SB according to your score. You can earn 300 SB for a perfect game.

- SB Mobile - SB Mobile brings Swagbucks to your mobile devices. On SB Mobile, you can enter swag codes, shop, complete surveys and watch videos.

- SB Answer - SB Answer is a mobile app that allows you to complete surveys for SB on your mobile device. You can also earn

SB by snapping photos of your receipts through the Answer app as well.

- SB Local - SB Local is a mobile app that shows you where you can earn cash back while shopping or dining locally. All you have to do is link your credit or debit card to your Swagbucks account, then you automatically earn SBs when you use that card to shop or dine at select stores and restaurants.
- SB Shop - The SB Shop app allows you to earn your SBs while shopping on your mobile devices.
- Swagbutton - Swagbutton is a browser app that allows you quick access to your Swagbucks account, shopping and videos. You can also redeem a swag code on

Swagbutton, rather than going to Swagbucks.com.

The following six SB apps are [Swagbucks](#) apps that you can use to earn SBs by watching videos on your mobile devices. Each of these apps shows a different topic of interest so that you can watch whatever videos interest you most and leave the rest.

- EntertaiNow - This app shows the latest entertainment news articles and videos.
- Sportly - This app shows sports entertainment and news videos.
- Lifestylz - This app shows entertainment and lifestyle content.
- MovieCli.ps - This app shows new movie clips.

- Indymusic - This app shows new Indy Music videos.
- Amped 360 - This app shows current action sports videos.

Tips and Tricks

Here's the fun part where I impart all my insider knowledge. Follow these tips and tricks and soon you will be a SwagMaster:

- I cannot stress this enough, Swagbucks is not a get rich quick scheme. While you can earn money and gift cards on Swagbucks, please don't quit your day job! I have earned $3 to $5 on a good day. Swagbucks will not bring in enough money to sustain you, but it is a fun way to earn a few extra bucks!
- Don't get disheartened if you are completing surveys and don't qualify. Some days you won't be able to qualify for any, and some days it will feel like you hit the jackpot. You will get 1SB (Up to 5

daily) just for attempting a survey, even if you don't qualify. Be patient and persistent and the SBs will come.

- On Swagbucks.com, the more you play, the more you earn. Be sure to participate in games like Swago and SwagIQ and Swagstakes. Not only are they fun, but you have the chance to bank some serious SB and other prizes link gift cards, cash and electronics!

- Take advantage of the special offers. I get in the habit of checking Swagbucks before I purchase anything online because I can usually find a deal that will get me some SB, be it cash back from shopping, or bonus SB for signing up for a service like Hulu or Blue Apron.

- Be sure to check out the offers from Swagbucks' trusted partners, such as Revenue Universe and Offer Toro. Sometimes their offers will get you more SBs than the offers from Swagbucks. You can earn lots of SB for downloading and playing games on mobile apps from Offer Toro.
- If you are watching videos on Swagbucks.com or via one of the mobile apps, you can play videos in the background while you do other things like dishes or folding laundry.
- If you go to Coupons.com through Swagbucks, you can get 2 SBs per coupon you print (Up to 50 per day) and 25 SBs per coupon when you redeem your printed coupons.

- You get 50 SBs just for installing the Swagbutton on your browser and can earn more SB from web searches by making Swagbucks your default browser. You can make Swagbucks your default browser under Swagbutton settings when you install Swagbutton on your computer.
- You must claim your monthly bonus each month or you will lose all your bonus SB! When your monthly bonus is available, it will show up under your daily goal meter and you can click it to claim your bonus SB.
- While playing SwagIQ, even if you are eliminated, you can still earn SB for answering questions correctly. Be sure to stay on until the end of the game to claim your SB!

- When playing Swago, you can only redeem your board for SBs once per game. For example, of you have one line and redeem that line for SBs, then you get another line, you won't be able to claim any SB for that second line. It is best to wait until the end of the game period to redeem for your SBs.

- You can use your SB to donate to charity. When you click on Redeem Swagbucks, click on Do Good and it will bring you to a page where you will be able to donate your SB to the charities such as UNICEF, Doctors Without Borders, Red Cross, etc.

- Be sure to like and/or follow Swagbucks on social media. Sometimes they post stealth swag codes that can't be found anywhere else. You can find Swagbucks

- on Facebook, Twitter, Instagram, Pinterest and YouTube.
- You can earn 300 SBs by referring your friends or family to [Swagbucks](). When you click on Refer and Earn, you will be able to invite people via email or social media or copy your special referral link to share with people via text or messenger. You can also get an extra 100 SBs when someone you refer adds the SwagButton on their laptop or desktop.
- You will get bonus SBs for completing your daily To Do List. Sometimes this isn't possible, for example if you can't qualify and complete a survey, but I can usually complete my To Do List several times per week.

- Don't forget to check out the SB Local app. You can earn SBs for shopping and dining at local businesses and restaurants when you sign up and connect your credit or debit card, then you automatically earn SB when you use that card to shop or dine at select stores and restaurants.

- Go to Swag Codes Spoiler, https://sc-s.com/ and click on notifications to find out how to get notified whenever there is a swag code available. You can sign up for notifications via Twitter, Facebook, RSS or Email.

- Check your Swagbucks Inbox daily and look through messages for easy ways to earn SB. Your inbox is located at the top of the page.

- When redeeming your SBs for gift cards, watch out for the sales. Sometimes you can pay less SBs than the gift card is worth, saving some SBs for a rainy day.

Conclusion

Now that you have read this book, you have now graduated the SwagMaster Academy, and you should be well on your way to becoming a SwagMaster! I hope that you have enjoyed this book as much as I have enjoyed writing it. I wish you all the best on your journey to becoming a SwagMaster.

References

Prodege Brands. (2019, February 14). Retrieved from Prodege: https://www.prodege.com/brands/

Swagbucks. (2019, February 13). Retrieved from Swagbucks: https://www.swagbucks.com

Swagbucks. (2019, February 14). *Swagbucks Blog*. Retrieved from Swagbucks: http://blog.swagbucks.com/

Wikipedia. (2019, February 13). Retrieved from Swagbucks: https://en.wikipedia.org/wiki/Swagbucks

About the Author

T. Cathers-Mitchell lives in northeastern Wisconsin with her wife and two children. She enjoys being a SwagMaster and writing about it, both in this book and in her blog, which you can find at http://swagmaster.home.blog.

www.ingramcontent.com/pod-product-compliance
Lightning Source LLC
Chambersburg PA
CBHW071203220526
45468CB00003B/1136